Jamie Shai And His Superpower

There is a hero in each of us, no matter how different we are.

WORDS MATTER
P U B L I S H I N G
OUR WORDS CHANGE THE WORLD

© 2022 by Lara Nathan. All rights reserved.

Words Matter Publishing
P. O. Box 1190
Decatur, Il 62522
www.wordsmatterpublishing.com

No part of this publication may be reproduced, stored in a retrieval system, or transmitted in any way by any means—electronic, mechanical, photocopy, recording, or otherwise—without the prior permission of the copyright holder, except as provided by USA copyright law.

ISBN: 978-1-953912-93-0

Library of Congress Catalog Card Number: 2022942824

To my family, Colin, Daniel, Jamie & Kyla,

you inspire me every day and are

truly the lights of my life.

Acknowledgements

To my family, who are my joy and pride.

To Words Matter Publishing for the opportunity to share Jamie's story and how he found his superpower.

Not long ago, a beautiful baby boy was born with green eyes and a sweetness that seemed so special.
They named him Jamie Shai.

7

A few months later, after his mom and dad realized he wasn't sitting or eating and couldn't hold himself up very well, they took him to a doctor who told them their beautiful baby boy had a problem with his muscles and that he probably wouldn't walk or talk or be able to use his muscles like most people can.

9

Jamie's mom and dad were heartbroken that their baby boy who was the most beautiful baby, wouldn't be able to do what most kids would. Jamie struggled to eat and hold his head up, his muscles would tighten and he would cry because he was frustrated. It was a very hard time for Jamie. His Mommy and Daddy would have done anything in the world to make his frustrations go away.

11

When Jamie started smiling, his mom and daddy's hearts lit up with so much joy. There was something truly special in his smile. Through his smile, they came to know Jamie, and he knew his Mommy and Daddy!

13

The more people they met, the more they realized how Jamie's smile lit up other peoples' faces and hearts. His beautiful eyes would look at a person and a smile as wide and bright as the sunrise would appear on his face and then a most warming, happy smile would appear on their faces too.

15

16

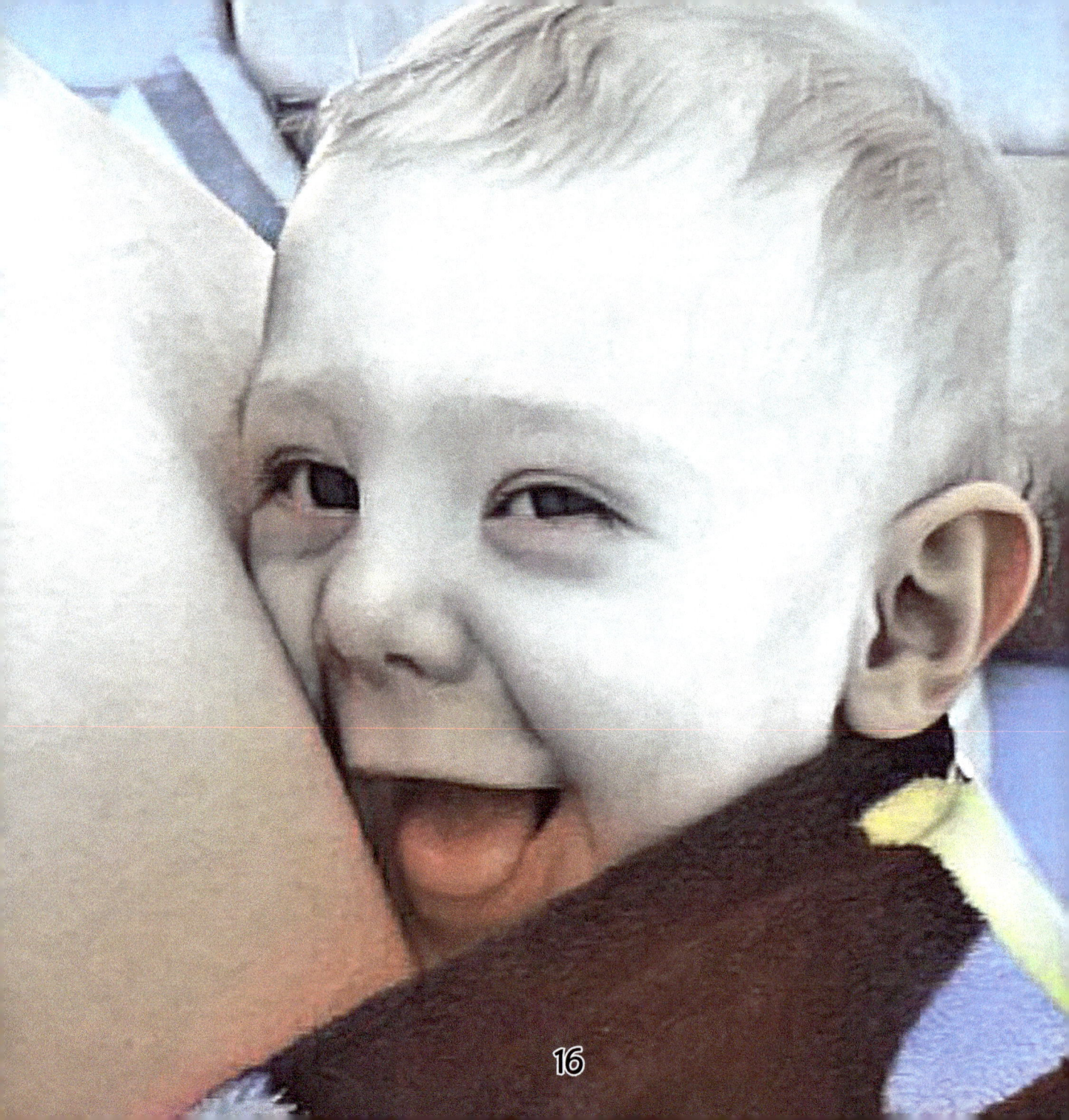

17

Other children would come up to Jamie, hold his hand, talk to him, smile at him and with him, and tell his mom and dad how special this little boy was.
Jamie had a way of making everyone around him **feel**.

19

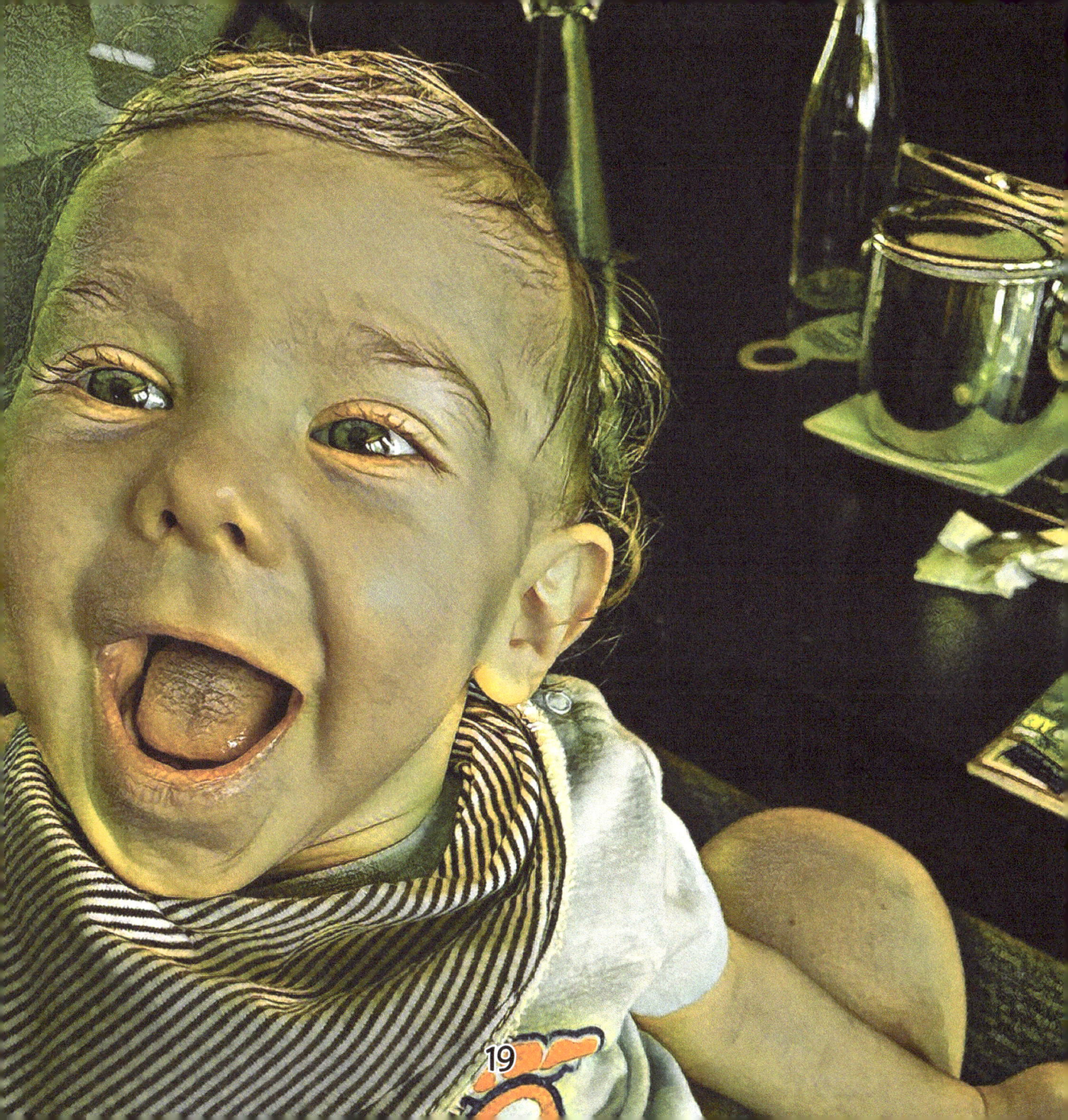

No matter where they went, to the grocery store, or on an airplane, on holiday, to school, people would stop to talk to Jamie, to smile back at him and tell Jamie's mom and dad how special and sweet Jamie was.

They were drawn to him. Something about his smile brightened the smiles of those around him.

21

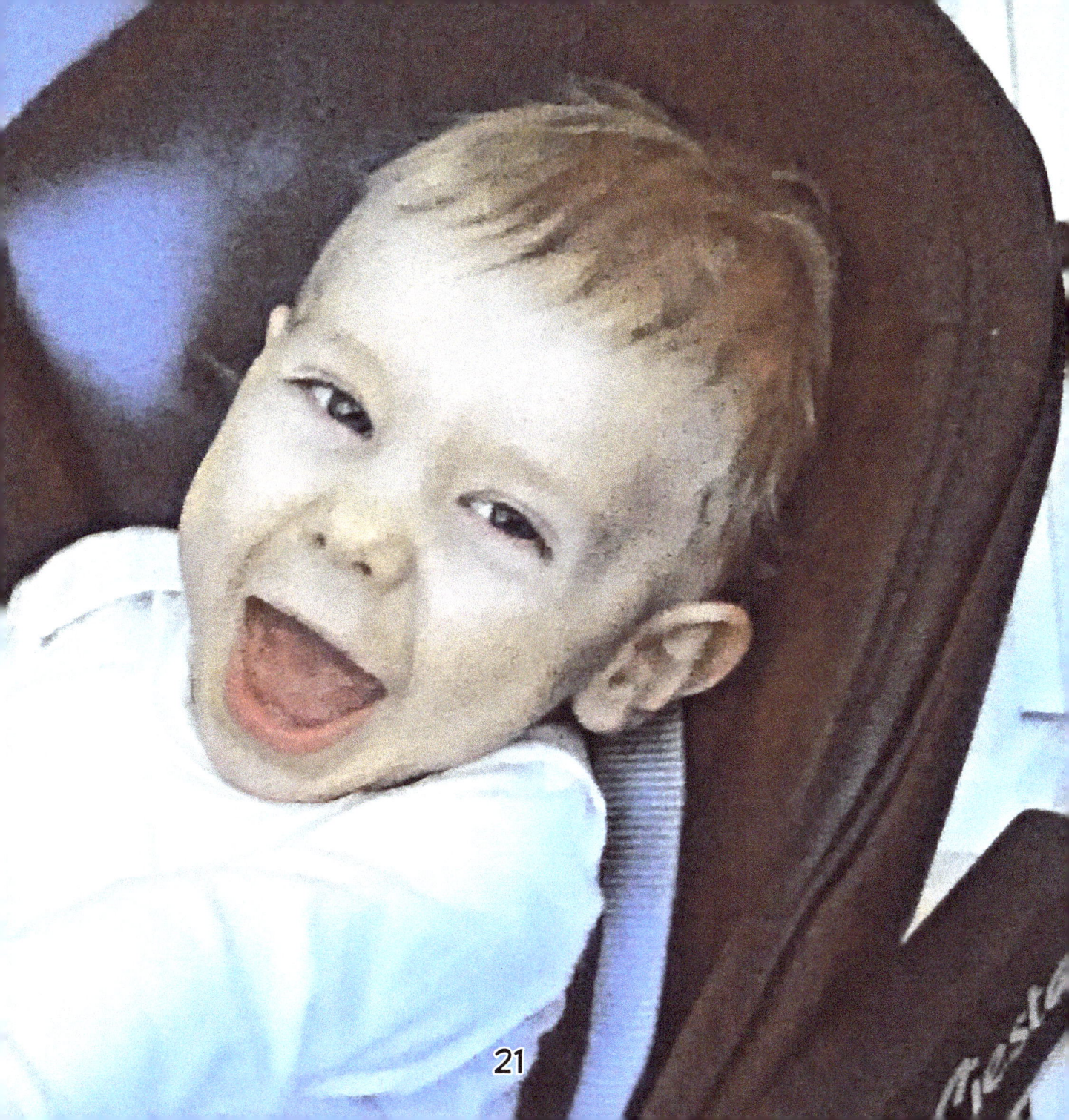

Soon his mom and dad realized that Jamie's smile was his superpower.

23

24

25

Jamie was able to make other people
smile no matter how young or old.
His smile made people happy,
his smile made people stop and look,
they couldn't help but come over to him.

27

28

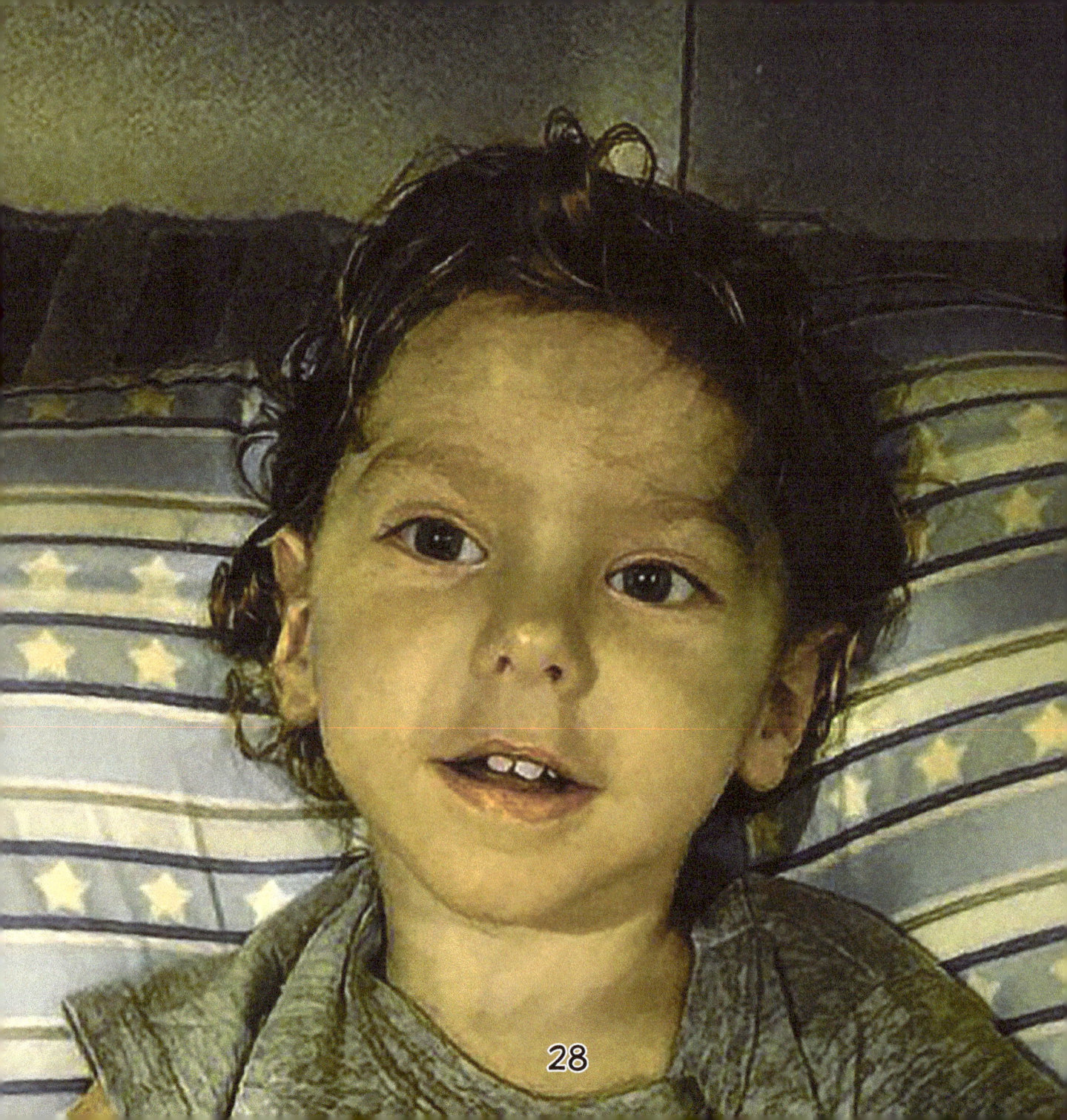

29

Curious children would always ask why he wasn't talking or why he was in a wheelchair, and Jamie would just smile his happiest, most beautiful smile, because he knew that it didn't matter that he couldn't walk or talk, and it didn't matter that he wasn't like most kids. What mattered is that he understood everything.

He knew his Mommy and his Daddy, and his brother and sister, he loved music and songs, and tv shows. He knew if you were happy or sad, and even mad or glad. But more than anything, he knew his smile brought smiles to everyone around him.

31

32

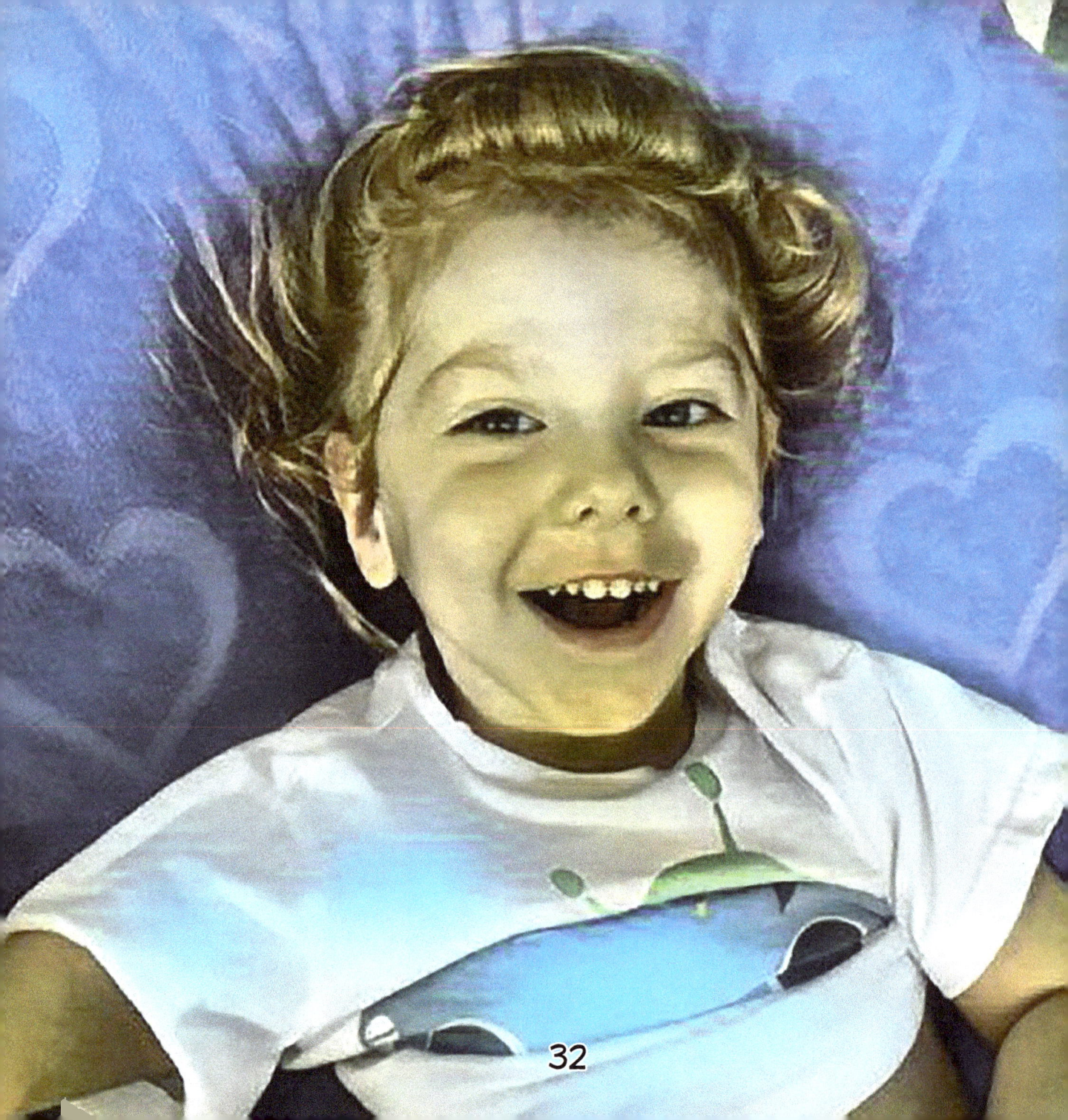

33

Jamie's older brother Daniel, had the most special bond with Jamie from the moment he was born. He felt like they were soulmates and that he could understand Jamie better than anyone. Jamie is his best friend and his most special younger brother.

35

Jamie's younger sister Kyla adores her brother and finds every opportunity to feed him, hold him, play with him and is most protective of, as she says, 'my Jamie Shai.'

37

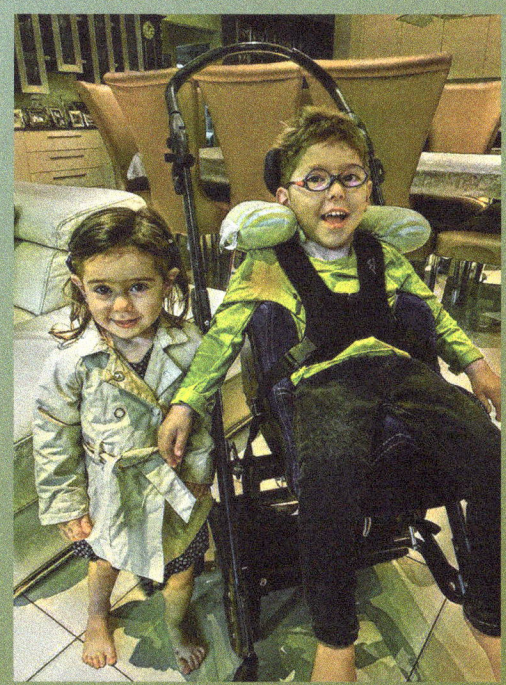

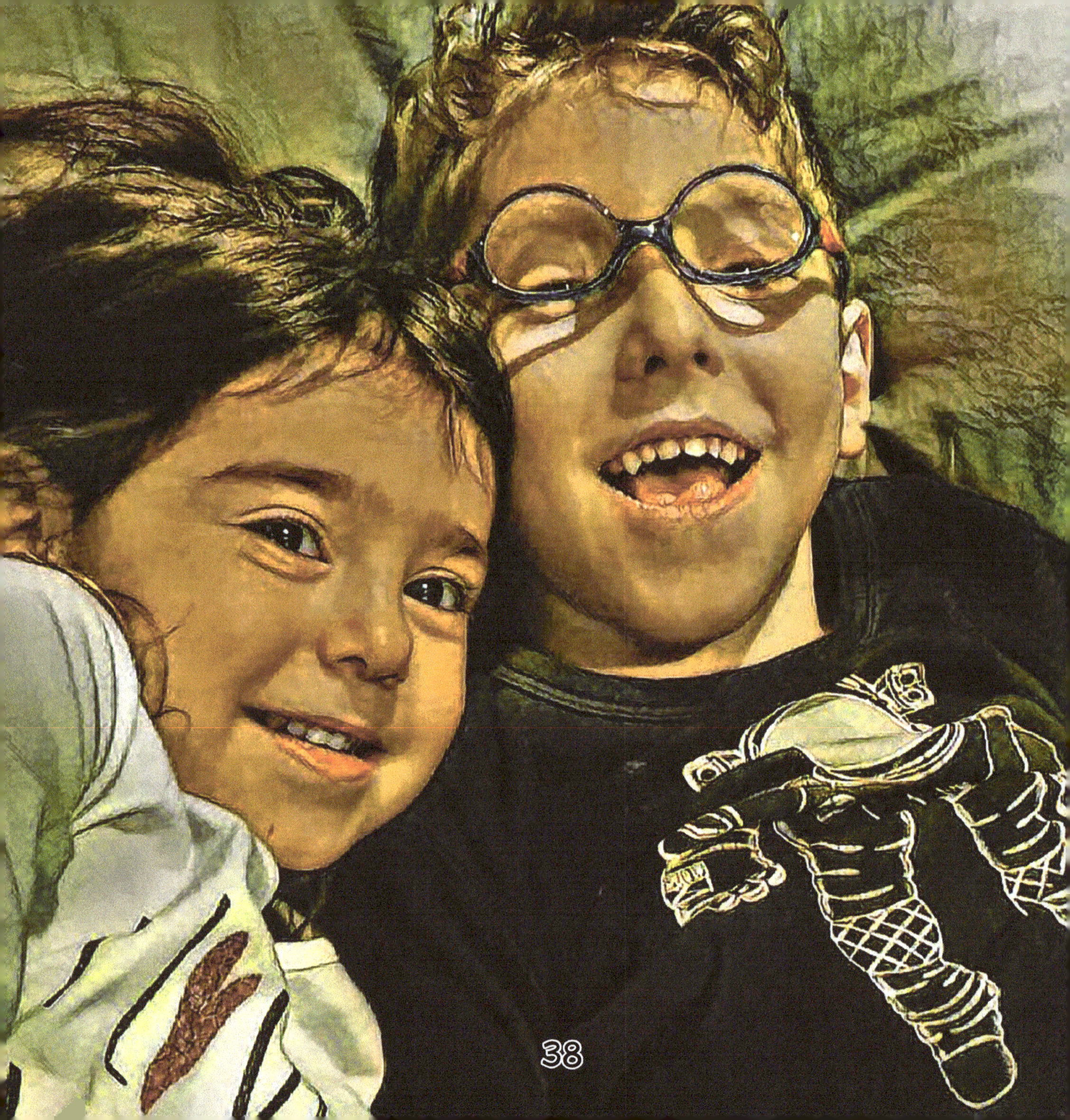

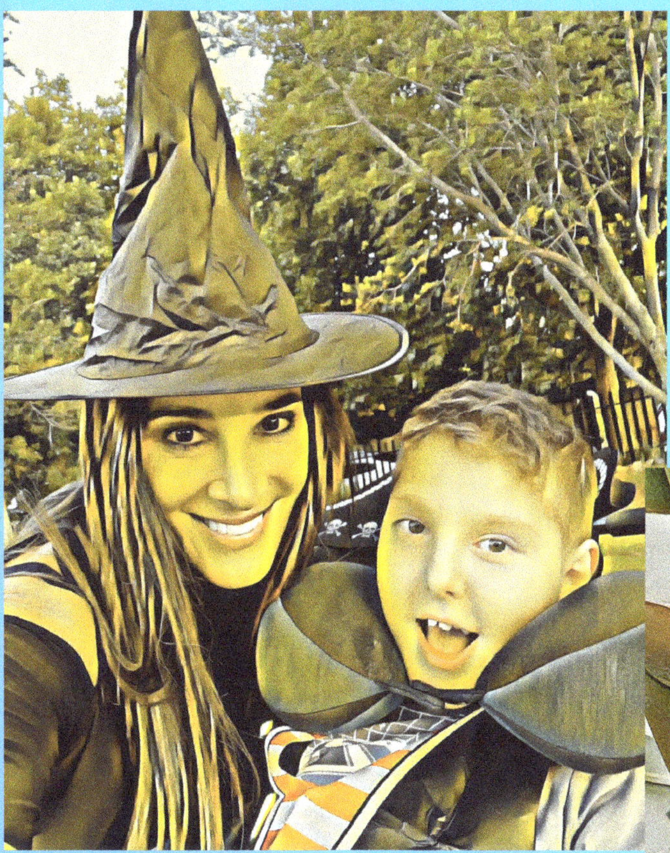

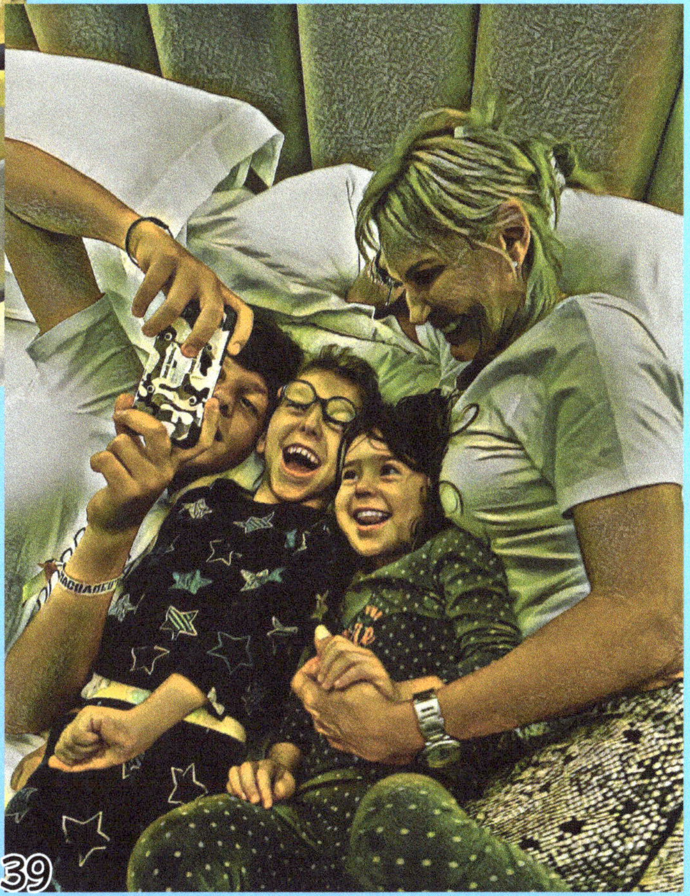

Jamie's smile even made people forget about a bad day, it made them remember what there is to smile about and be happy about, and Jamie knew that he was making a difference just by smiling, and that being different didn't matter, it mattered that his smile made a difference to others...

He found his superpower.

41

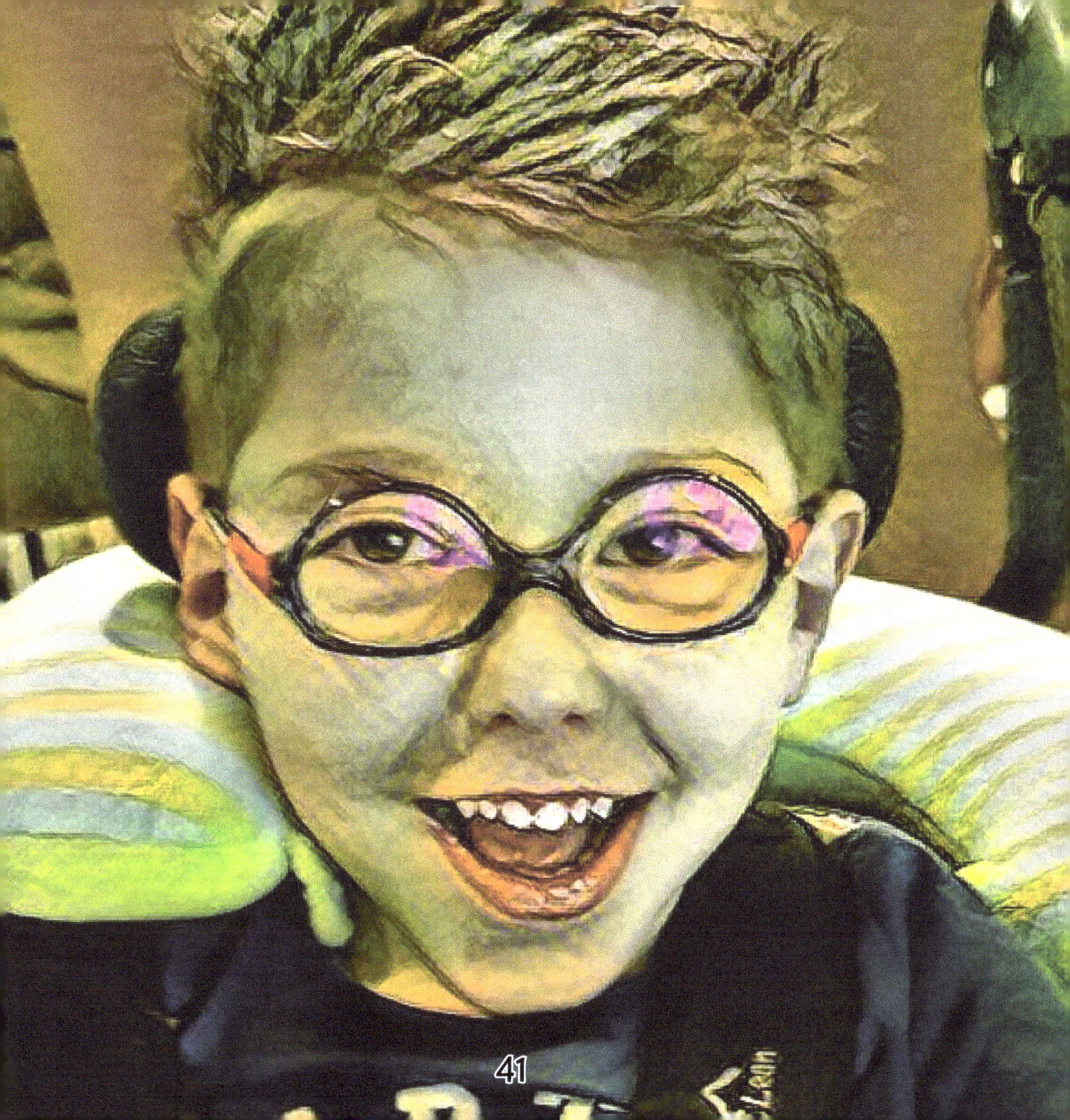

About the Author

Months after a traumatic birth, Jamie Shai was diagnosed with Cerebral Palsy. Unable to eat, walk or talk, it was a devastating time, yet out of such challenges came Lara's greatest gift and greatest inspiration. Jamie Shai, they later learned was incredibly intelligent, and he found his superpower and a way to share his joy. They say if you make a difference to one life, you make a difference to all - Jamie makes a difference daily to those he meets and those he is surrounded by and in doing so, makes a difference in our world.

Lara has been a successful real estate professional in Johannesburg, South Africa, for the last 20 years and has also starred in the first reality TV property show in South Africa, Listing Jozi. The inspiration for this book was of course Lara's son, Jamie Shai, who inspires her daily and has taught life lessons she has been privileged enough to learn. There is a superhero in all of us, no matter what challenges we face.

CPSIA information can be obtained
at www.ICGtesting.com
Printed in the USA
LVHW072005030423
743358LV00006B/656